HOUSTON
TEXANS

BY J. T. NORMAN

SportsZone

An Imprint of Abdo Publishing
abdopublishing.com

abdopublishing.com

Published by Abdo Publishing, a division of ABDO, PO Box 398166, Minneapolis, Minnesota 55439. Copyright © 2017 by Abdo Consulting Group, Inc. International copyrights reserved in all countries. No part of this book may be reproduced in any form without written permission from the publisher. SportsZone™ is a trademark and logo of Abdo Publishing.

Printed in the United States of America, North Mankato, Minnesota
042016
092016

Cover Photo: Damian Strohmeyer/AP Images
Interior Photos: Damian Strohmeyer/AP Images, 1; Tony Gutierrez/AP Images, 4-5, 15; David Drapkin/AP Images, 6; Eric Gay/AP Images, 7; Ed Betz/AP Images, 8-9; Thomas B. Shea/Icon SMI 750/Newscom, 10-11; Robert E. Klein/AP Images, 12-13; Charlie Riedel/AP Images, 14; Bill Kostroum/AP Images, 16-17; Dave Einsel/AP Images, 18-19, 20, 22-23; Wade Payne/AP Images, 21, 26; Smiley N. Pool/Houston Chronicle/AP Images, 24-25; Jim Mahoney/AP Images, 27; Patric Schneider/AP Images, 28-29.

Editor: Patrick Donnelly
Series Designer: Nikki Farinella

Cataloging-in-Publication Data
Names: Norman, J. T., author.
Title: Houston Texans / by J. T. Norman.
Description: Minneapolis, MN : Abdo Publishing, [2017] | Series: NFL up close | Includes index.
Identifiers: LCCN 2015960424 | ISBN 9781680782189 (lib. bdg.) | ISBN 9781680776294 (ebook)
Subjects: LCSH: Houston Texans (Football team)--History--Juvenile literature. | National Football League--Juvenile literature. | Football--Juvenile literature. | Professional sports--Juvenile literature. | Football teams--Texas--Juvenile literature.
Classification: DDC 796.332--dc23
LC record available at http://lccn.loc.gov/2015960424

TABLE OF CONTENTS

J. J.'S JUMP

J. J. Watt was surprised to find the ball in his hands. The burly defensive lineman of the Houston Texans had jumped to knock down a pass by Andy Dalton of the Cincinnati Bengals. But Watt did not knock it down. He caught it instead.

Watt sprinted toward the end zone with the interception. He raised both hands as he crossed the goal line. He saluted the big home crowd. The Houston fans went crazy.

It happened just before halftime on January 7, 2012, in the Texans' first-ever playoff game.

J. J. Watt celebrates after his huge play against the Bengals.

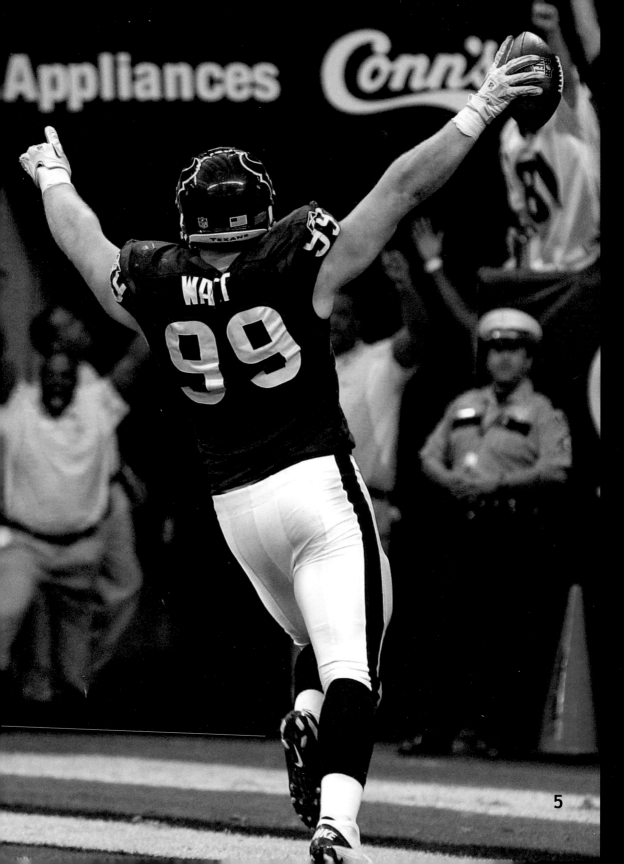

The Texans finally made it to the playoffs in their 10th season. They faced the Cincinnati Bengals in the first round. Watt's big play gave the Texans a 17-10 halftime lead. Wide receiver Andre Johnson caught a 40-yard touchdown pass in the second half. The Texans' defense forced an interception. Running back Arian Foster added a 42-yard touchdown run in the fourth quarter.

With a 31-10 victory, the Houston Texans had shown they could go toe to toe with any team in the National Football League (NFL).

The home crowd had plenty to celebrate as the Texans beat Cincinnati in the first playoff game in team history.

Arian Foster
tiptoes into the
end zone against
the Bengals.

FAST FACT
In 2011, the Texans' defense ranked second in the NFL in yards allowed and fourth in points allowed.

BACK TO HOUSTON

The city of Houston lost its NFL team in 1997. The Houston Oilers had played there since 1960. But the team's owner moved them to Tennessee.

Local businessman Bob McNair quickly began working on a plan to bring the NFL back to Houston. The city agreed to build a new stadium. The league awarded an expansion team to McNair in 1999.

David Carr, *left*, stands with NFL commissioner Paul Tagliabue after Houston made Carr their first-ever draft pick.

FAST FACT

The Texans were given the first overall pick in the 2002 NFL Draft. They selected quarterback David Carr from Fresno State.

FAST FACT

Before the Texans shocked the Cowboys, only one other expansion team had ever won its first game. The Minnesota Vikings beat the Chicago Bears in 1961.

Linebacker Jay Foreman, *left*, and the Texans' defense kept Hall of Fame running back Emmitt Smith bottled up in Houston's first regular-season game.

The Texans began play in 2002. Like all expansion teams, they were a mix of young, unproven players and veterans who nobody else wanted. Coach Dom Capers led them to a 4-12 record in their first season. It was not a great showing, but the season did have a memorable start.

Houston played its first regular-season game against the Dallas Cowboys. A national television audience watched Carr throw two touchdown passes. The defense played tough. The Texans pulled off a 19-10 upset victory.

THE EARLY YEARS

The first season revealed one big problem with the Texans. David Carr was sacked 76 times. That was by far the most in the NFL. The Texans did not develop an offensive line to protect Carr. He was sacked 249 times in 76 career games with Houston.

David Carr spent a lot of time on the ground in his five years with the Texans.

FAST FACT

David Carr's younger brother, Derek Carr, also played quarterback at Fresno State. He was the Oakland Raiders' second-round draft pick in 2014.

It looked like the Texans were about to turn the corner in 2004. They swept the division-rival Tennessee Titans and Jacksonville Jaguars on their way to a 7-9 record. Second-year receiver Andre Johnson had 1,142 receiving yards and was picked for the Pro Bowl.

FAST FACT

Rookie running back Domanick Davis rushed for 1,031 yards in 2003. Fans voting at NFL.com named him the NFL Rookie of the Year.

Domanick Davis had an impressive rookie year for the Texans.

Andre Johnson goes head over heels to score a touchdown against the Minnesota Vikings.

But that success turned out to be short-lived. The Texans won just two games in 2005. Carr was sacked 68 times, and the defense allowed the most points in the league. Coach Dom Capers was fired. Houston replaced him with Gary Kubiak, a longtime offensive assistant for the Denver Broncos.

Kubiak got the Texans pointed in the right direction. In 2006, they won their final two games to finish 6-10. Linebacker DeMeco Ryans led the team in tackles and was named the NFL Defensive Rookie of the Year. Once again, the Texans appeared to be a team on the upswing.

Mario Williams, *top*, and DeMeco Ryans team up to tackle running back Kevan Barlow of the New York Jets in 2006.

TEXANS RISING

In 2007, the Texans won as many games as they lost for the first time. Then they went 8-8 again in 2008. Former Atlanta Falcons backup Matt Schaub was brought in to replace David Carr. Schaub battled through injuries, but backup Sage Rosenfels led Houston to five wins over those two seasons. One of those victories came late in the 2008 season as the Texans beat the Jacksonville Jaguars in their first appearance on *Monday Night Football*.

The Texans and backup
quarterback Sage Rosenfels
were flying high in 2008.

FAST FACT

Texans running back Steve
Slaton led all rookies with
1,282 rushing yards in 2008.

In 2009, Schaub stayed healthy for 16 games, and the Texans got the results they were hoping for. He led the NFL with 4,770 passing yards. Even better, Schaub and the Texans posted a 9-7 record. Their first winning season did not end with a playoff berth, but Texans fans finally had reason to be optimistic.

FAST FACT

Linebacker Brian Cushing was named the NFL Defensive Rookie of the Year in 2009.

Brian Cushing pressures New England quarterback Brian Hoyer.

Matt Schaub, *left*, put up big numbers for the Texans in 2009.

Running back Arian Foster became a star during the 2010 season. He opened the season by posting a team-record 231 rushing yards in a 34-24 win over the Indianapolis Colts. And he did not slow down all season. Foster led the NFL with 1,616 rushing yards and 16 touchdowns. He also came up big in the passing game with 66 catches for 604 yards.

The Texans won four of their first six games. But after their bye week, they hit a big slump and finished with eight losses in their last 10 games. The first trip to the playoffs would have to wait one more year.

Arian Foster, 23, breaks away from the Indianapolis Colts' defense on his record-setting day in 2010.

23

PLAYOFF PUSH

Fans had reason to worry after the Texans started the 2011 season 3-3. But then running back Arian Foster scored three touchdowns in a big win at Tennessee. That started a seven-game winning streak that gave Houston its first division title.

However, quarterback Matt Schaub was lost for the season with a foot injury. Rookie T. J. Yates took over and led the Texans to the playoffs. Yates threw a 6-yard touchdown pass to receiver Kevin Walter with two seconds left in the game to beat the Cincinnati Bengals and clinch a spot in the postseason. After beating the Bengals again in the first round of the playoffs, Houston lost to the Baltimore Ravens 20-13.

Kevin Walter scores a touchdown to give the Texans a 20-19 win at Cincinnati and clinch their first division championship.

The next year was even better for the Texans. Schaub came back and had another big season. Foster ran for 1,424 yards and 15 touchdowns. Houston won 11 of its first 12 games. The Texans forced six turnovers in a win at Tennessee to clinch another playoff spot. Two weeks later, they beat the Indianapolis Colts to wrap up their second straight division title.

Houston beat Cincinnati again in the playoffs before losing to the New England Patriots in the second round. However, J. J. Watt was named the NFL Defensive Player of the Year after posting 20.5 quarterback sacks.

Linebackers Whitney Mercilus, 59, and Connor Barwin close in on Titans quarterback Jake Locker in Houston's playoff-clinching victory in 2012.

FAST FACT

In 2012 the Texans won two overtime games in five days. They beat the Jaguars on November 18 and then beat the Lions in Detroit on Thanksgiving Day.

J. J. Watt intimidated opponents throughout his award-winning 2012 season.

A NEW BEGINNING

After two great years, the bottom dropped out in 2013. The Texans went 2-14, losing their last 14 games. Injuries played a huge role in the collapse. Matt Schaub, Arian Foster, and Brian Cushing each missed at least half of the season after getting hurt. Coach Gary Kubiak was fired before the season ended.

His replacement, Bill O'Brien, led the Texans to 9-7 records in each of his first two seasons. J. J. Watt continued his dominant play. He had 20.5 sacks and earned his second Defensive Player of the Year Award in 2014. He followed that with 17.5 sacks as the Texans won their division again in 2015.

FAST FACT

Defense carried the Texans in 2015. They gave up the third-fewest total yards and passing yards in the NFL. In six of their victories, the Texans held their opponents under 10 points.

DeAndre Hopkins caught 111 passes for 1,521 yards and a team-record 11 touchdowns in 2015.

TIMELINE

1999
The NFL awards businessman Bob McNair and Houston a new team.

2002
The Texans win their first game, beating the visiting Dallas Cowboys 19-10 on September 8.

2009
The Texans win their last four games to record their first winning record at 9-7.

2010
Arian Foster runs for a team-record 231 yards during the season-opener, a 34-24 win over the Indianapolis Colts on September 10.

2011
Houston wins its division and reaches the playoffs for the first time.

2012
The Texans beat the Cincinnati Bengals 31-10 on January 7 in their first playoff game.

2014
J. J. Watt wins the NFL Defensive Player of the Year Award for the second time in three seasons.

2015
The Texans win seven of their final nine games to finish with a 9-7 record and another division title.

GLOSSARY

BYE
A week during the season in which a football team does not play a game.

DIVISION
A group of teams that help form a league.

EXPANSION
When a league grows by adding new teams.

INTERCEPTION
When a defensive player catches a pass intended for an offensive player.

PLAYOFFS
A set of games after the regular season that decides which team will be the champion.

RIVAL
An opponent with whom a player or team has a fierce and ongoing competition.

SACK
A tackle of the quarterback behind the line of scrimmage before he can pass the ball.

TURNOVER
Loss of the ball to the other team through an interception or fumble.

VETERAN
A player who has played many years.

INDEX

ABOUT THE AUTHOR

J. T. Norman grew up watching football on television. He lives in Texas and can't wait to play backyard football with his kids.